The story of:

_____

A baby has a special
way of adding joy
in every single day.

AUTHOR UNKNOWN

Scripture quotations are taken from

The Holy Bible, New International Version®, NIV®. Copyright © 1973, 1978, 1984, 2011 by Biblica, Inc.® Used by permission. All rights reserved worldwide.

The ESV® Bible (The Holy Bible, English Standard Version®), copyright © 2001 by Crossway, a publishing ministry of Good News Publishers. Used by permission. All rights reserved.

The New American Standard Bible®, © 1960, 1962, 1963, 1968, 1971, 1972, 1973, 1975, 1977, 1995 by The Lockman Foundation. Used by permission. (www.Lockman.org).

The New King James Version®. Copyright © 1982 by Thomas Nelson, Inc. Used by permission. All rights reserved.

Cover by Nicole Dougherty

Artwork © by Ginger Chen

BUNDLE OF JOY
Copyright © by Harvest House Publishers
Published by Harvest House Publishers
Eugene, Oregon 97402
www.harvesthousepublishers.com

ISBN 978-0-7369-6941-3

Printed in China

16 17 18 19 20 21 22 23 24 / RDS-JC / 10 9 8 7 6 5 4 3 2 1

Bundle of Joy

HARVEST HOUSE PUBLISHERS
EUGENE, OREGON

Congratulations on your little bundle of joy!

You are probably exhausted, elated, overwhelmed, filled with joy…and experiencing every other emotion imaginable. Whether this is your first child or the one who gives you a baker's dozen, this gift from God has just changed your world. You want to be a good parent, maybe even a perfect parent—the kind of parent who records every single thing this sweet little person does.

Let's get one thing straight. You will be a great parent *and* you probably won't be able to capture every funny or tender moment. There are simply too many. That's the blessing of a baby!

So don't worry about recording every little detail or milestone. Instead, be in the moment with your little one. Open this book when you can for encouragement on your journey and the opportunity to record glimpses of your child's story.

Most importantly, know that you are not missing a thing when you are staring at your sleeping baby, listening to sweet giggles, or getting down on the floor to give the one hundredth horsey ride of the day. Those are the moments you will remember forever.

Enjoy your precious bundle of joy!

Every child begins the world again.

HENRY DAVID THOREAU

Happy Birthday, Little One!

_____

Birth Date

_____

Arrival Time

_____

Original Due Date

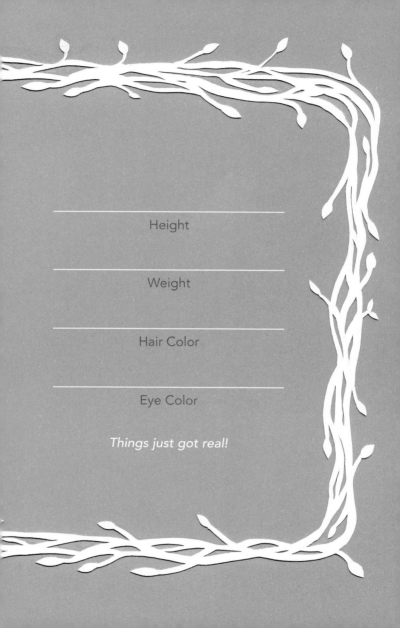

_____
Height

_____
Weight

_____
Hair Color

_____
Eye Color

Things just got real!

Describe how you felt the moment you heard your baby's first cry.

_____

_____

_____

_____

_____

_____

_____

_____

_____

_____

_____

_____

_____

Every good and perfect gift is from above.

What was the first thing
you noticed about your baby?

Use this page as a guest book or list
who visited you in the hospital.

Children are
living jewels
dropped
unstained
from heaven.

ROBERT POLLOK

What was the
weather like on your
baby's birthday?

....

....

....

Tell your baby's birth story.

*Include the important details, such as speeding
tickets, winter storms, acts of heroism, etc.*

_____

_____

_____

_____

_____

_____

_____

_____

_____

_____

_____

_____

_____

_____

_____

You formed
my inward parts;
you knitted me
together in my
mother's womb.

THE BOOK OF PSALMS

Does your little one have a birthmark or unique feature?

_____

_____

_____

_____

Trace your baby's
hand today.

_____

Date/Age

Children are
the hands by
which we take
hold of heaven.

HENRY WARD BEECHER

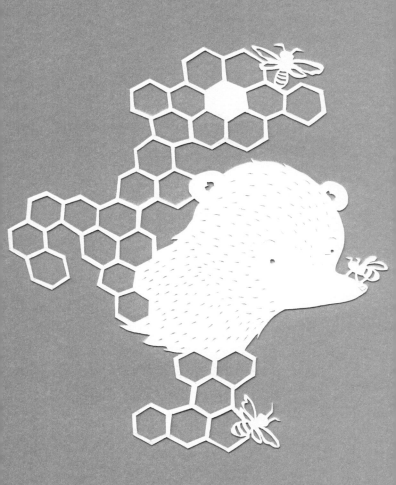

What makes your baby smile?

_____

_____

_____

_____

If it's a funny face you make, take a selfie of it!

Describe your
baby's personality
using one word.

_____

Behold, children are
a gift of the LORD,
the fruit of the womb
is a reward.

THE BOOK OF PSALMS

How has the color of your little one's eyes changed?

The color may change more than once, so come back and note continuing changes.

Share an embarrassing
parenting moment.

Don't worry, your secret is safe here.

How did you pick
your baby's name?

_____

_____

_____

_____

_____

Were there any other
names in the running?

_____

_____

_____

A mother's arms are made of tenderness, and children sleep soundly in them.

VICTOR HUGO

Record the
longest stretch of time
you have been awake
with your baby.

Bonus points for every hour past 24.

Take your baby
for a family walk.
Find a memento
—a pretty leaf or flower
or a shiny penny—
and tuck it inside
this book.

What is something
you are looking forward to
sharing with your little one
when he/she is old enough?

_____

_____

_____

_____

_____

A favorite movie, food, activity, etc.?

For this child I prayed.

Take a moment to pray for your baby and record your prayer.

_____

_____

_____

_____

_____

_____

_____

_____

_____

_____

_____

_____

_____

_____

Every child born
into the world is a
new thought of God,
an ever fresh and
radiant possibility.

KATE DOUGLAS WIGGIN

Trace your baby's footprint today.

If you have the footprint card you received at the hospital, tuck it in here.

_____

Date/Age

Take a selfie with
your baby and
paste or tape it
to this page.

Twinkle,
twinkle,
little star,
do you know
how loved
you are?

AUTHOR UNKNOWN

How does your little one feel about bath time?

_____

_____

_____

_____

On a scale of 1 to 10, how wet do you end up?

1   2   3   4   5   6   7   8   9   10

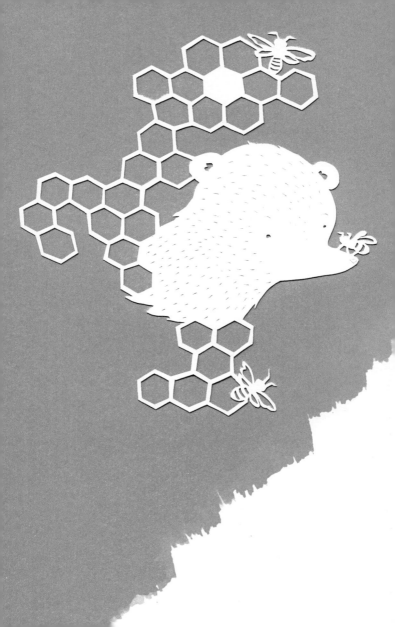

First and favorite foods.

Did curiosity get the better of you?
How did it taste?

_____

_____

_____

_____

_____

_____

_____

_____

_____

_____

_____

_____

Take a trip to a nearby beach, lake, or river. Record a special moment.

_____

_____

_____

_____

_____

_____

_____

_____

_____

_____

_____

_____

If you have a picture of it, tuck it in here.

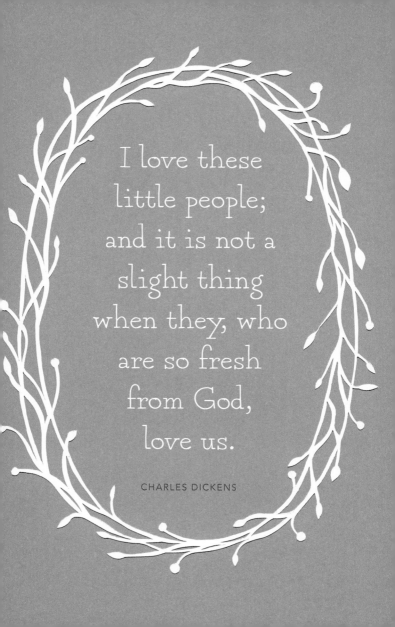

I love these
little people;
and it is not a
slight thing
when they, who
are so fresh
from God,
love us.

CHARLES DICKENS

Record a moment when you
were completely overwhelmed
with love for your child.

What are some of your little one's favorite words or phrases?

_____

_____

_____

_____

_____

_____

_____

_____

_____

_____

_____

Start a family tradition today!

*Perhaps a special lullaby, evening walk,
family pizza night, etc.*

God created boys,
Full of spirit and fun,
To explore and conquer,
To romp and run.

AUTHOR UNKNOWN

Little girls bring
such delight with
hearts so warm and
smiles so bright!

AUTHOR UNKNOWN

Share the best parenting advice you have received.

Share the weirdest parenting advice you have received.

More importantly, did you follow it?

_____

_____

_____

_____

_____

_____

_____

_____

_____

_____

_____

_____

We find
delight in the beauty
and happiness of
children that makes
the heart too big
for the body.

RALPH WALDO EMERSON

Jot down a thought for today of
a special moment or memory.

_____

_____

_____

_____

_____

_____

_____

_____

_____

_____

_____

_____

Take a trip to
a local zoo or aquarium.
Which animals did
your kiddo respond to?

_____

_____

_____

_____

_____

What are your
little one's
favorite songs?

Children sing,
ever sing,
Loudest praise to
God our King.

FANNY CROSBY

Grab a crayon or two and
let your child draw a picture
or simply color on this page.

Date/Age

Does your kiddo
have a favorite
stuffed animal
or blanket?

_____

_____

_____

Of all
created things,
the loveliest and
most divine
are children.

WILLIAM CANTON

Now the fun really begins!

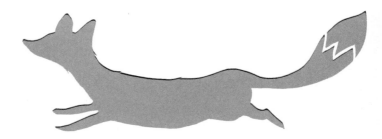

First steps...
when/where?

Is there anything your
child does that you know
you should probably stop,
but it's just too cute?

_____

_____

_____

_____

_____

_____

_____

_____

_____

_____

_____

Girl,
n. A giggle with
glitter on it.

AUTHOR UNKNOWN

A boy is Truth with
dirt on its face,
Beauty with a cut
on its finger,
Wisdom with bubble
gum in its hair, and
the Hope of the future
with a frog in its pocket.

AUTHOR UNKNOWN

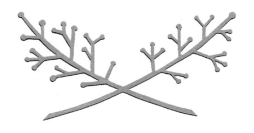

Does your little
one have a nickname?
Where did it come from?

_____

_____

_____

_____

_____

Is your
kiddo affectionate?
Or do hugs and kisses
feel like a special occasion?

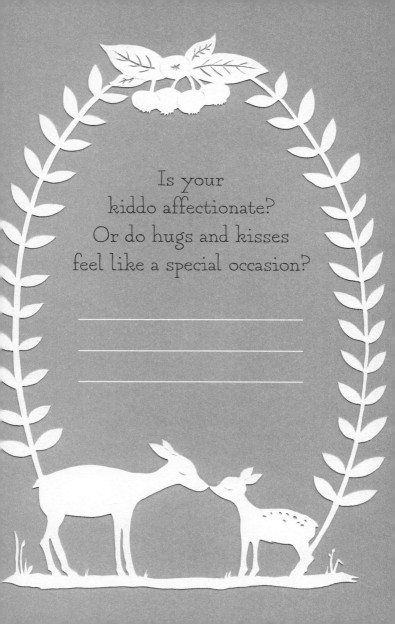

Start children off on
the way they should go,
and even when they
are old they will not
turn from it.

THE BOOK OF PROVERBS

Take a moment to pray for your little one and record your prayer.

_____

_____

_____

_____

_____

_____

_____

_____

_____

_____

_____

_____

_____

What word or phrase does your child say that cracks you up?

Come back to this page and add to it!

Create an adventure,
complete with a map
and buried treasure,
for your kiddo.
Tuck the map between
these pages.

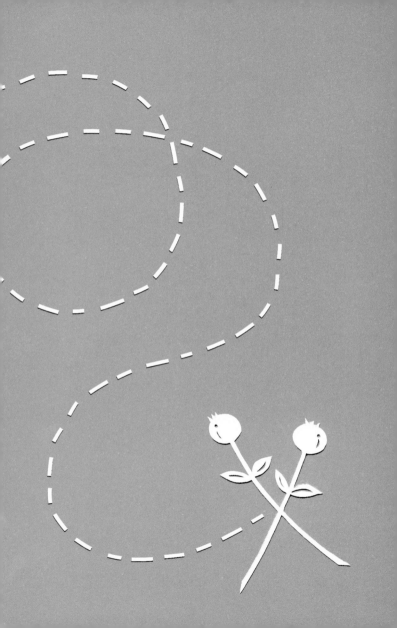

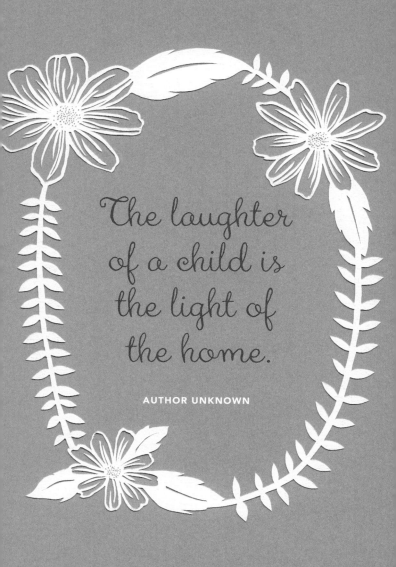

The laughter
of a child is
the light of
the home.

AUTHOR UNKNOWN

When your child plays make-believe, who does your child pretend to be?

---

*Take a blanket and make a cape,
a saddle, a princess skirt, etc.*

Turn on some music
and have a dance party
with your kiddo.
What songs did
you dance to?

What's a favorite moment
or routine you have each day
with your little one?

Nap time is a perfectly acceptable answer.

Create a
living room picnic.
Put a tablecloth on
the floor, grab some
fun finger foods,
and enjoy!

Record a parenting fail.

_____

_____

_____

_____

_____

_____

_____

_____

_____

_____

_____

_____

_If you can't think of one, that's okay.
You'll be back soon. ;)_

I may
not be perfect,
but when I look
at my children,
I know that I
got something
in my life
perfectly right.

AUTHOR UNKNOWN

What physical characteristics
does your little one share
with Mom or Dad?

What personality characteristics
does your little one share
with Mom or Dad?

_____

_____

_____

_____

_____

_____

_____

Positive. Think positive!

As a mother
comforts her
child, so will
I comfort you.

THE BOOK OF ISAIAH

Take a moment to pray for your
little one and record your prayer.

_____

_____

_____

_____

_____

_____

_____

_____

_____

_____

_____

_____

_____

Does your child have
a favorite storybook?

_____

_____

_____

Have a family backyard
campout or living room
slumber party.
Set up a tent and grab
flashlights and sleeping bags.
S'mores should definitely
be involved.

A rose can say
"I love you,"
Orchids can enthrall,
But a weed bouquet
in a chubby fist,
Yes, that says it all.

AUTHOR UNKNOWN

Trace your baby's hand today.

Refer back to the earlier print and compare!

_____

Date/Age

Record a piece of advice or wisdom
that you would like to pass along
to your little one someday.

_____

_____

_____

_____

_____

_____

_____

_____

_____

_____

_____

_____

_____

Let the children come to me; do not hinder them, for to such belongs the kingdom of God.

THE BOOK OF MARK

Congratulations— you finished!

What an accomplishment (especially when you throw in extreme sleep deprivation).

We hope you were able to record some of the special moments without any added guilt or stress. Even better, maybe you were able to spend some intentional time with your little one.

The fun doesn't have to stop here. You can go back and add to these pages, noting the dates for the different entries. Or start your own memory journal using this book for ideas.

Enjoy every day with your kiddo. As you know, the months will go by too fast!

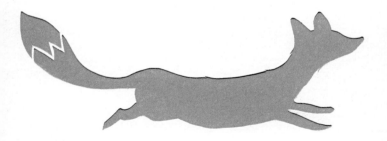